CAREER EXPLORATION

Flight Attendant

by Rosemary Wallner

Consultant:
Debra M. Blondeau
Flight Attendant
Sun Country Airlines

CAPSTONE BOOKS
an imprint of Capstone Press
Mankato, Minnesota

Capstone Books are published by Capstone Press
151 Good Counsel Drive, P.O. Box 669, Mankato, Minnesota 56002
http://www.capstone-press.com

Library of Congress Cataloging-in-Publication Data
Wallner, Rosemary, 1964–
    Flight attendant/by Rosemary Wallner.
    p. cm.—(Career exploration)
    Includes bibliographical references and index.
    Summary: Introduces the career of flight attendant, discussing educational
requirements, duties, work environment, salary, employment outlook, and possible
future positions.
    ISBN 0-7368-0489-7
    1. Flight attendants—Vocational guidance—Juvenile literature. [1. Flight
attendants—Vocational guidance. 2. Vocational guidance.] I. Title. II. Series.
HD8039.A43 W35 2000
387.7'42—dc21   99-053794
                                                                          CIP

Editorial Credits
Leah K. Pockrandt, editor; Steve Christensen, cover designer; Kia Bielke, production
    designer and illustrator; Heidi Schoof, photo researcher
Photo Credits
Archive Photos, 9
Jeff Greenberg/Photo Agora, 18
Mark Reinstein/FPG International LLC, 39
Northwest Airlines, 10, 13
Sean McCoy, cover, 6, 22, 28, 31, 33
Unicorn Stock Photos/Jeff Greenberg, 21, 25, 47
Uniphoto, 36
Visuals Unlimited/Jeff Greenberg, 14, 17, 34, 40

**Special thanks to personnel of Sun Country Airlines for their assistance with
this book.**

1 2 3 4 5 6 05 04 03 02 01 00

Table of Contents

Fast Facts

Career Title	Flight Attendant
O*NET Number	68026
DOT Cluster (Dictionary of Occupational Titles)	Service occupations
DOT Number	352.367-010
GOE Number (Guide for Occupational Exploration)	09.01.04
NOC Number (National Occupational Classification-Canada)	643
Salary Range (U.S. Bureau of Labor Statistics and Human Resources Development Canada, late 1990s figures)	U.S.: $12,800 to $40,000 Canada: $13,000 to $43,300 (Canadian dollars)
Minimum Educational Requirements	U.S.: high school diploma Canada: high school diploma
Certification/Licensing Requirements	U.S.: none Canada: none

Subject Knowledge	Customer and personal service; psychology; geography; public safety and security; transportation
Personal Abilities/Skills	Speak clearly; talk easily with all kinds of people to put them at ease; use judgment and reasoning to cope with emergencies such as sudden illness, accident, or interrupted service; perform a variety of activities; change activities frequently and sometimes without notice
Job Outlook	U.S.: faster than average growth Canada: fair
Personal Interests	Accommodating: interest in catering to the wishes of others, usually on a one-on-one basis
Similar Types of Jobs	Travel agent or travel counselor; ship purser; passenger attendant; camp counselor; maritime crew member

Chapter 1

Flight Attendant

Flight attendants are members of a flight crew. Other crew members include a pilot, co-pilot, and flight engineer. A flight engineer assists the other pilots. A flight engineer monitors and operates many of the airplane instruments and systems. Flight crews work to make sure the airplanes and passengers are ready to fly.

Where Flight Attendants Work

Most flight attendants work for commercial airlines. These companies own and operate many airplanes. Some flight attendants work for large companies that own airplanes or helicopters.

The Federal Aviation Administration (FAA) oversees airplane safety. Airlines must follow FAA rules. One rule states that airlines must have one flight attendant for every 50 airplane seats.

Most flight attendants work for commercial airlines.

The number of flight attendants needed for each flight depends on the size of the airplane. Small planes may only need one or two attendants. Some large planes may have as many as 16 flight attendants on board.

History

The first flight attendants were men. They were called couriers. These couriers were the sons of ship, railroad, or other business owners who financed airlines.

In the 1920s, airlines hired stewards. These men worked on planes. Their duties included serving food to passengers.

In the 1930s, airlines began to hire women. Airline executives believed female attendants would reassure passengers of air travel safety. The first airline attendants were called stewardesses. In Canada, a stewardess also was called an air hostess.

Early stewardesses had many duties. They helped passengers board planes and served meals and beverages such as juice and soft drinks. They also put fuel in the plane, loaded baggage, and mopped the cabin floor. The cabin is a section of the plane for passengers, crew, or cargo. Many

Airlines began to hire female flight attendants in the 1930s.

airlines required stewardesses to be registered nurses as well. These stewardesses needed to be able to provide medical care if needed.

Airlines had many rules that affected stewardesses. For example, stewardesses had age, height, and weight requirements. They also had to be unmarried women. During the 1970s, airlines began calling stewardesses flight attendants. Men were allowed to become flight attendants in the mid-1970s.

Flight attendants serve food to passengers.

Flight Attendants' Duties

Flight attendants make sure passengers are safe and comfortable during airplane flights. Flight attendants serve passengers in several ways.

Flight attendants' main duty is to make sure that passengers follow safety regulations. Before takeoff, flight attendants check that all passengers are seated with their seat belts fastened. Flight attendants explain the airplane safety equipment before every flight. They also show passengers where the exits are located.

Passengers need to know where the exits are in case there is an emergency landing.

Flight attendants' most important responsibility is to provide safety to passengers. For example, flight attendants help passengers during turbulence. This atmospheric condition is caused by swirling winds that create strong air resistance. These winds cause a plane to fly up and down quickly. The motion sometimes scares passengers and may cause air sickness. Flight attendants make sure passengers stay in their seats with their seat belts fastened. Passengers who leave their seats during turbulence may be injured. Flight attendants also must sit down with their seat belts fastened. Both passengers and flight attendants must stay seated until the captain turns off the seat belts sign.

Flight attendants also provide personal service to passengers. Flight attendants help passengers store carry-on items in overhead compartments. They bring pillows and blankets to passengers who need them. Flight attendants often serve food and beverages to passengers. They also help passengers who become ill or who have medical problems.

Flight attendants are busy before, during, and after each flight. They make sure passengers find their seats before the plane takes off. They walk up and down the aisles and talk with passengers during the flight. Flight attendants help passengers find their carry-on bags at the end of the flight. After each flight, flight attendants write reports about the flight. They also make lists of supplies that need to be replaced.

Flight Attendants at Work

Flight attendants often live near their airline's home base. Most airlines have their base of operations in large cities. These include New York, Minneapolis, Chicago, and Los Angeles. Flight attendants may be away from their home base one-third of their working time.

Flight attendants work varied hours. They sometimes work at night and on holidays and weekends. Flight attendants usually fly about 75 to 85 hours a month. They also work on the ground about 40 to 50 hours a month. On the ground, they prepare for flights, greet passengers, and write reports. Flight attendants have about 15 days off each month depending on their schedules.

Flight attendants work on both domestic and international flights. Domestic flights are between two cities in the same country. International flights are between cities in different countries. An international flight might take off from New York

Flight attendants may work on domestic and international flights.

City and land in London, England. Some flight attendants may work on just one type of flight.

Flight attendants must wear uniforms. Most uniforms consist of a white shirt with pants or a skirt. Some uniforms include a vest, sweater, or jacket. Most flight attendants must purchase their uniforms. They are required to wear their uniforms while they are working. Many airlines pay flight attendants an allowance to dry clean their uniforms.

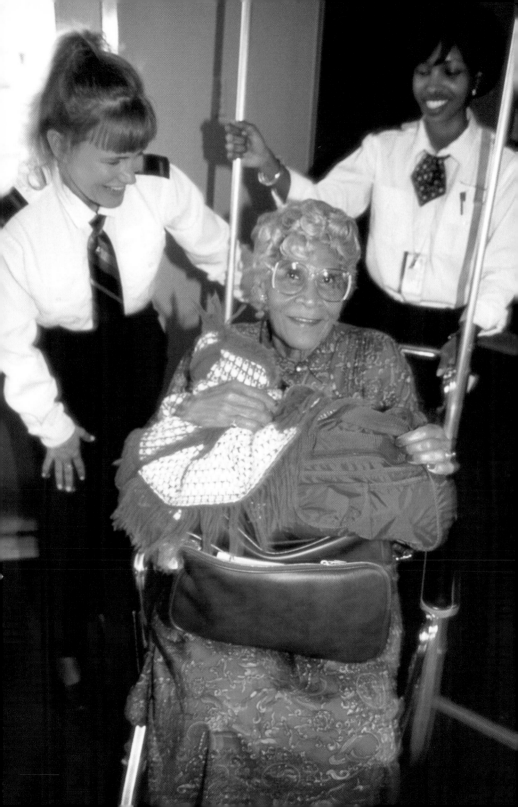

Chapter 2

Day-to-Day Activities

Flight attendants perform a variety of duties. They work before, during, and after each flight. One of their important responsibilities begins when passengers board the airplane.

Preflight Duties

Flight attendants meet with the flight crew one hour before the plane is scheduled to depart. This meeting is called the preflight briefing session. The pilot in command of the airplane is the crew captain. The captain discusses what the weather will be like during the flight. The captain also tells the flight crew how long the flight will last.

Flight attendants check the cabin after the preflight briefing session. They make sure

Flight attendants sometimes assist passengers who need extra help.

everything is ready for the flight. They have about 45 minutes to prepare the cabin before passengers board the airplane. During that time, flight attendants do a preflight check. They check that all emergency equipment is present and works. They make sure there are enough pillows and blankets. They adjust the cabin lights. They also work with the flight engineer about the air-conditioning and heating system. On some airplanes, flight attendants adjust the cabin temperature.

Flight attendants make sure there are enough supplies on the plane. They check the first-aid kit. This kit contains bandages, a thermometer, and other supplies to treat minor medical problems. Flight attendants also make sure the plane has enough food, beverages, and other supplies on board.

Boarding Passengers
Flight attendants greet passengers near the airplane doors. They check tickets and help passengers find their seats. Flight attendants help passengers put away coats and carry-on items. They also assist people who need extra help. These may include elderly or physically disabled people.

Flight attendants meet for preflight briefing sessions.

Flight attendants also perform important duties right before the plane takes off. They check the number of passengers against the flight manifest to make sure the numbers match. The manifest is the passenger list. Flight attendants shut and arm the entry doors. To arm the doors, flight attendants engage the escape slides attached to the doors. They do this by moving a lever or securing a bar to brackets in the plane's floor. This allows the slides to operate if the emergency doors are opened.

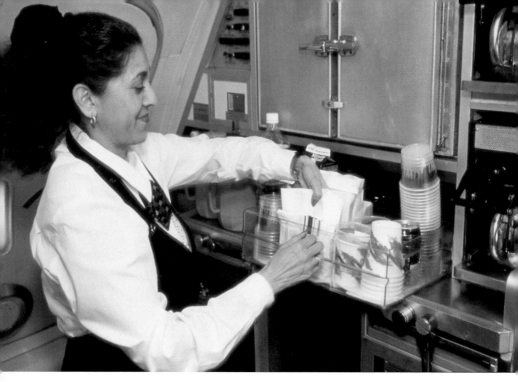

Flight attendants prepare items to be served in the galley.

Flight attendants walk up and down the aisles. They check that passengers have fastened their seat belts. They make sure passengers put their seatbacks and tray tables in the upright and locked position. They check that carry-on items are in overhead compartments or under seats.

Flight attendants also tell passengers how to use the airplane's emergency equipment. They show them how to use the oxygen masks. These masks supply passengers with oxygen if the plane loses air pressure. Flight attendants also point out the exits to the passengers.

During the Flight
Flight attendants have much work to do once the plane is in the air. On some flights, they serve meals to passengers. They may need to heat these precooked meals in the kitchen. An airplane kitchen also is called a galley. Flight attendants serve the meals from carts they move through the aisles. Flight attendants also serve beverages to passengers. On some flights, flight attendants serve only snacks and beverages.

Flight attendants make sure passengers are comfortable. They offer magazines, blankets, and pillows to passengers. Flight attendants also answer questions about the plane and flight.

Landing Duties
Flight attendants walk up and down aisles often when the plane gets closer to its destination. The captain announces an "approach check" to tell flight attendants that the destination is near. Flight attendants then collect any remaining used cups, plates, and utensils from passengers. They tell passengers to fasten their seat belts. They

also tell passengers to put their seatbacks and tray tables in an upright and locked position. They make sure carry-on bags are put back in the overhead compartments or under the seats.

Flight attendants help passengers after the plane lands. They make sure passengers have their belongings. They help passengers get items from overhead bins. Flight attendants stand near the exit as passengers leave the plane.

Attendants on international flights may give passengers information about customs regulations. Customs is the checkpoint at a country's airport where officials make sure passengers are not carrying anything illegal. They may provide other airport information. Flight attendants also may explain flight information or instructions to passengers who speak another language.

Flight attendants have other duties after passengers leave the plane. They write down any supplies that need to be restocked for the next flight. Supplies may include pillows, paper towels, and other items. Flight attendants note any equipment that needs fixing. They write a report about any medical or other problems that

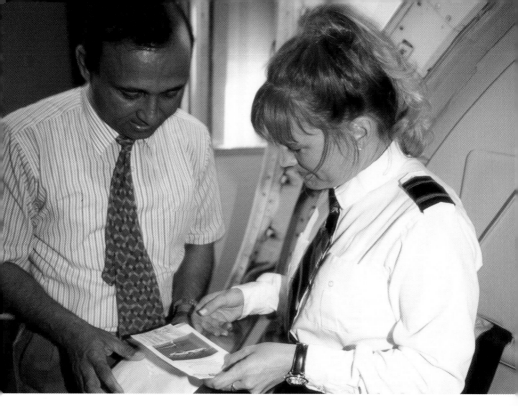

Flight attendants may give passengers airport information.

occurred during the flight. They give any articles
left behind on the airplane to the gate agent.

Flight attendants sometimes do not return to
their home base after each flight. They may have a
layover in another city before leaving. The layover
may last for a few hours or overnight. Airlines pay
for hotel rooms when flight attendants are on
layovers. Airlines also give a per diem for meals.
A per diem is an amount of money for food.

Chapter 3

The Right Candidate

Flight attendants need a variety of skills and interests. They should like to travel and work with people. They must be able to handle stressful situations. Flight attendants should communicate well and remain calm in emergencies.

Interests

Flight attendants work in cities around the world. They must be self-sufficient. They must be able to deal with being away from their families and friends for periods of time. They must adapt well to new places. They sometimes spend several nights in a row in different cities.

Flight attendants should enjoy working with people. They should want to help others. They also should be concerned about others' health and comfort. Flight attendants work with many types

Flight attendants should enjoy working with people.

of people. Some people are friendly and polite. Others may be nervous or angry. Flight attendants must remain calm and pleasant no matter what kind of people they encounter.

Skills

Flight attendants must handle unusual or emergency situations calmly and efficiently. For example, they must be able to handle a passenger's sudden illness. They must be able to deal with an emergency landing. Flight attendants must remain calm and use good judgment under all circumstances.

Flight attendants need good communication skills. They must speak clearly to passengers and other crew members. Flight attendants must be able to put passengers at ease.

Flight attendants must work well in teams. They must follow instructions from other crew members. They also share information with crew members.

Flight attendants and other flight crew members represent an airline to the public. They must be well-groomed, friendly, capable, and confident.

Health

Flight attendants must be in good health. They should have good eyesight and hearing. They must

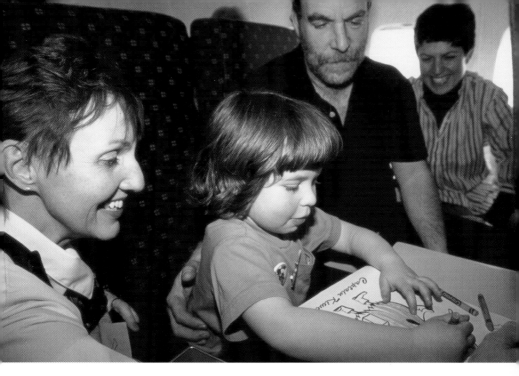

Flight attendants must remain calm and pleasant.

pass a physical examination. Flight attendants
must be able to stand for long periods of time.
They also must be able to push and pull about
150- to 250-pound (70- to 110-kilogram) carts.

Flight attendants in good health often work
many hours during a flight. They must be able
to keep their balance while the plane is flying.
They must not be afraid of heights or tight
spaces. They must be able to walk through the
plane's aisles even when there is turbulence.

Flight attendants must be alert. Airlines
randomly test flight attendants for drugs.

Skills

Workplace Skills
Yes / No

Resources:
- Assign use of time .... ☑ ☐
- Assign use of money .... ☑ ☐
- Assign use of material and facility resources .... ☑ ☐
- Assign use of human resources .... ☐ ☑

Interpersonal Skills:
- Take part as a member of a team .... ☑ ☐
- Teach others .... ☑ ☐
- Serve clients/customers .... ☑ ☐
- Show leadership .... ☑ ☐
- Work with others to arrive at a decision .... ☑ ☐
- Work with a variety of people .... ☑ ☐

Information:
- Acquire and judge information .... ☑ ☐
- Understand and follow legal requirements .... ☑ ☐
- Organize and maintain information .... ☑ ☐
- Understand and communicate information .... ☑ ☐
- Use computers to process information .... ☑ ☐

Systems:
- Identify, understand, and work with systems .... ☑ ☐
- Understand environmental, social, political, economic,
  or business systems .... ☑ ☐
- Oversee and correct system performance .... ☐ ☑
- Improve and create systems .... ☐ ☑

Technology:
- Select technology .... ☐ ☑
- Apply technology to task .... ☑ ☐
- Maintain and troubleshoot technology .... ☐ ☑

Foundation Skills

Basic Skills:
- Read .... ☑ ☐
- Write .... ☑ ☐
- Do arithmetic and math .... ☑ ☐
- Speak and listen .... ☑ ☐

Thinking Skills:
- Learn .... ☑ ☐
- Reason .... ☑ ☐
- Think creatively .... ☑ ☐
- Make decisions .... ☑ ☐
- Solve problems .... ☑ ☐

Personal Qualities:
- Take individual responsibility .... ☑ ☐
- Have self-esteem and self-management .... ☑ ☐
- Be sociable .... ☑ ☐
- Be fair, honest, and sincere .... ☑ ☐

Airlines want to make sure flight attendants are fit and healthy to work.

Flight attendants must be able to handle stress. It can be stressful to work with demanding passengers or to fly in bad weather. Flight attendants sometimes must serve meals quickly on short flights. Flight attendants must remain pleasant regardless of how tired or stressed they become.

Job Hazards

Flight attendants can be injured or become ill due to their job. Some get back injuries from standing for long periods of time. Pushing and pulling heavy carts and lifting heavy items also can cause back injuries. Some flight attendants are injured by items that fall out of overhead compartments. Some have medical problems because they breathe a plane's recycled air for long periods of time.

Some flight attendants also experience irregular sleeping and eating patterns. This is often due to their varied schedules and travel through different time zones. A time zone is a region in which the same time is used. Flight attendants' bodies may not adjust well to these changes in time.

Chapter 4

Preparing for the Career

People must train to become flight attendants. High school graduates may apply for jobs at airlines. People at the airlines train new flight attendants. These people teach the flight attendants skills they need to perform their jobs.

High School Education

People who want to become flight attendants should take a variety of high school classes. These include geography, social studies, and health classes. In geography classes, students learn about people and places from around the world. Students learn about what is happening in the world in social studies classes. Health classes teach students how to stay fit and healthy. Students also should

People must train to become flight attendants.

take psychology classes. This science studies the human mind, emotions, and behavior.

Students should develop good communication skills. Classes such as English and speech help students develop these skills. Students also may study a foreign language. Most flight attendants who work on international flights speak at least one foreign language.

The Application Process

People who want to become flight attendants must earn a high school diploma. They then can apply to airlines for jobs. Flight attendants must be at least 19 years old. Many airlines prefer to hire people who have some college education. Many airlines also prefer to hire people who have worked with the public.

Some airlines also have other requirements for flight attendants. Most U.S. domestic airlines require that attendants be U.S. citizens or have an immigration visa. These documents allow people from another country to work in the United States. Most international airlines require attendants to speak one or more foreign languages well.

Flight attendant trainees should have good communication skills.

Flight attendant applicants must pass a medical exam and meet certain physical standards. Airlines require attendants to be at least 5 feet 2 inches (157 centimeters) tall in order to reach the overhead bins. Applicants' weight also should be in proportion to their height. Applicants who are selected by airlines then enter the airlines' training programs.

The Training Program

Newly hired flight attendants are called trainees. Trainees must complete four to six weeks of training at an airline's flight training center. Some airlines provide housing for their trainees. They may pay trainees a small amount of money for expenses. Some airlines do not have their own training centers. These airlines send their trainees to other airlines' training centers.

Trainees learn a great deal about planes and passengers at the training center. Trainees learn what to do in an emergency. They learn how to evacuate an airplane. Flight attendants must know how to remove passengers from an airplane quickly, properly, and safely. Trainees learn how to survive if a plane lands in water. They also learn about security issues such as how to handle hijackers. Hijackers are people who illegally take control of airplanes.

Flight attendants may need to help sick or injured passengers. Trainees learn how to give passengers first aid and cardiopulmonary resuscitation (CPR). CPR is a method of restarting a heart that has stopped beating.

Trainees learn about how an airline operates. They learn about flight regulations and duties. Trainees learn about company policies. They learn

Trainees learn about airplane safety at training centers.

the proper dress code. They also learn about physical considerations such as overall health and fitness. They learn the kinds of equipment aircraft use. Trainees for international flights also learn about passports and customs regulations.

Trainees practice in mock-up sessions toward the end of their training. These sessions take place in airplanes. Trainees serve food to people acting as passengers. They practice evacuation methods on land and in water. Video cameras

Flight attendants review how to handle emergencies during retraining courses.

record their actions. Later, the trainees watch the recordings. The tape shows them how they can improve their job performance.

After Training
Airlines place trainees on reserve status after they complete the training program. Flight attendants with reserve status fill in for crew members who are sick or on vacation. They must be available on short notice. They usually remain on reserve

from six months to six years. How long a flight attendant stays on reserve status depends on the airline.

Flight attendants not on reserve status can bid on regular flight assignments. Each month, flight attendants indicate which flights they want to work. Assignments also are called lines. Flight attendants bid their lines on a computer system.

Flight assignments are based on seniority. Flight attendants with the most years of experience get to choose their lines first. They might pick flights close to their home base. They also might pick daytime or weekday flights. Newer flight attendants often must work flights farther away from their home base.

Retraining

Flight attendants must complete a retraining course every year. This course takes 12 to 14 hours to complete. It includes a review of what to do in emergencies. The course also reviews how to make passengers comfortable and satisfied.

During retraining, flight attendants learn about new equipment and security concerns. They also learn from airplane accidents or other problems that have occurred.

Chapter 5

The Market

Flight attendants' salaries and advancement opportunities vary with their experience and skills. Experienced flight attendants have more job opportunities.

Salary

Flight attendants' salaries depend on many factors. Experienced flight attendants earn higher salaries than new flight attendants. Flight attendants who work certain routes and on larger airplanes also may earn more.

All flight attendants receive a base salary. This salary is to work a certain number of flight hours each month. Flight attendants are guaranteed between 67 and 85 hours each month. They receive more money for flight hours over the minimum number. They also receive extra pay for overnight and international flights.

Flight attendants' salaries increase with experience.

Flight attendants' salaries vary in the United States and Canada. The salary range for flight attendants in the United States is $12,800 to $40,000 per year. The average salary for flight attendants is about $27,000. The salary range for flight attendants in Canada is $13,000 to $43,300 per year. The average salary for flight attendants in Canada is $27,900.

Benefits

Flight attendants have the same benefits as other airline employees. They receive paid vacations, sick leave, and medical and life insurance. They also may participate in retirement programs.

Flight attendants also receive air travel benefits. Flight attendants' close family members can fly for free or for a low cost.

Most flight attendants belong to a union. This group seeks better working conditions, treatment, and pay for workers. A union helps negotiate wage contracts with airlines. To negotiate, two or more individuals or groups discuss items until they reach an agreement.

Job Outlook

Job opportunities for flight attendants are favorable. The number of applicants is in balance with the number of job openings. People who have

Flight attendants have favorable job opportunities.

experience dealing with the public may have more
job opportunities.

Job openings occur for several reasons. These
include when flight attendants leave the field or
accept a different job with the airline. Most flight
attendants stay with their jobs for many years. But
some attendants may get tired of traveling and
spending time away from home.

The job outlook for flight attendants varies
between the United States and Canada. In the
United States, the need for flight attendants is

Flight attendants may become lead attendants.

expected to grow faster than average. In Canada, the need for flight attendants is fair.

Advancement Opportunities

Flight attendants may advance as they gain experience. Experienced flight attendants may become lead or first flight attendants. These flight attendants also are called pursers. Lead attendants oversee the work of other flight attendants. They make announcements and serve meals and beverages to the pilots. Most lead attendants also perform the same duties as other flight attendants on flights.

Some flight attendants transfer to other airline jobs. They may become recruiters. These people encourage high school or college students to become flight attendants. Some flight attendants may become reservation agents or ticket agents. These people help passengers purchase airplane tickets. Some flight attendants become in-flight supervisors or trainers of new flight attendants.

Flight attendants who seek jobs at another airline must start as entry-level flight attendants. They must apply, interview, and train with that airline. They usually receive the same salary and seniority status as new flight attendants.

Related Careers

People who like to travel and work with others have many job opportunities. They may become ship pursers or passenger attendants. People in these occupations help passengers on cruise ships.

Other people may become travel agents or travel counselors. These individuals help people make travel plans.

Flight attendants' job opportunities will increase as the travel industry grows. Flight attendants will be needed as more people use air transportation.

Words to Know

airline (AIR-line)—a company that owns and flies airplanes; airlines carry passengers and freight by air.

cabin (KAB-in)—a section of an airplane for the passengers, cargo, or crew

cardiopulmonary resuscitation (kar-dee-oh-PUHL-muh-nair-ee ree-se-se-TAY-shuhn)—a method of restarting a heart that has stopped beating

customs (KUHSS-tuhms)—a checkpoint at a country's airport where officials make sure passengers are not carrying anything illegal

destination (dess-tuh-NAY-shuhn)—the place where an airplane is headed during a flight

evacuate (i-VAK-yoo-ate)—to move away from an area that is dangerous

galley (GAL-ee)—the kitchen on an airplane

hijacker (HYE-jak-ur)—a person who takes over an airplane illegally

layover (LAY-oh-vur)—to land for a few hours or overnight before taking off again

manifest (MA-nuh-fest)—a list of passengers on a plane

turbulence (TUR-byuh-luhns)—irregular atmospheric motion that causes up and down air currents

To Learn More

Bock, Becky S. *Welcome Aboard! Your Career as a Flight Attendant.* Englewood, Colo.: Cage Consulting, 1998.

Cosgrove, Holli, ed. *Career Discovery Encyclopedia.* Vol. 3. Chicago: Ferguson Publishing, 2000.

Eberts, Marjorie, Linda Brothers, and Ann Gisler. *Careers in Travel, Tourism, and Hospitality.* VGM Professional Careers. Lincolnwood, Ill.: VGM Career Horizons, 1997.

Lobus, Catherine Okray. *Careers as a Flight Attendant: Flight to the Future.* New York: Rosen Publishing, 1996.

Paradis, Adrian A. *Opportunities in Airline Careers.* VGM Opportunities. Lincolnwood, Ill.: VGM Career Horizons, 1997.

Useful Addresses

Air Transport Association of America
1301 Pennsylvania Avenue NW
Suite 1100
Washington, DC 20004-1701

Association of Flight Attendants
1275 K Street NW
Suite 500
Washington, DC 20005-4090

Association of Professional Flight Attendants
1004 West Euless Boulevard
Euless, TX 76040

Canadian Tourism Human Resource Council
170 Laurier Avenue West
Suite 1104
Ottawa, ON K1P 5V5
Canada

Internet Sites

Association of Flight Attendants
http://www.flightattendant-afa.org

**Association of Professional Flight
Attendants (APFA)**
http://www.apfa.org

Career Awareness—Flight Attendant
http://hrdc-drhc.gc.ca/career/directions98/
eng/flight.shtml

**Human Resources Development Canada—
Occupations in Travel and Accommodation**
http://www.hrdc-drhc.gc.ca/JobFutures/
english/volume1/643/643.htm

**Occupational Outlook Handbook—Flight
Attendants**
http://stats.bls.gov/oco/ocos171.htm

Index